T0247283

A Field of Voices

Hymns for Worship

James E. Clemens & David Wright

Church Publishing
NEW YORK

For Alex, Lena, Hannah, and Ethan,
who sing and make us want to write songs.

The publishers gratefully acknowledge permission to reproduce texts and tunes granted by publishers listed as copyright holders below each hymn. Contact information for these publishers appears in the notes and/or acknowledgments pages of this volume.

Music engraving by James E. Clemens
Book design by Linda Brooks
Cover by Laurie Klein Westhafer
Used with permission.

ISBN: 978-0-89869-653-0

First published in 2007 by
Table Round Press
Dayton, Virginia
www.tableroundpress.com

Published in 2010 by Church Publishing, Incorporated.
445 Fifth Avenue
New York, New York 10016

www.churchpublishing.org

5 4 3 2 1

Contents

PREFACE

Church Publishing is delighted to offer *A Field of Voices: Hymns for Worship* by James E. Clemens and David Wright. This collection by such fresh voices in music and poetry is a welcome addition to the hymnody of the church for its worship, meditation, proclamation, and prayer. The broad sampling of musical styles represented here and the thoughtful texts based on scripture and discernment are in keeping with the demand for a diversity of voices among contemporary Christians. New and emerging congregations will find these hymns useful in their less formal gatherings and established communities will be fed from this bounty as well.

Of the thirty selections more than a third can be taught and sung without the aid of printed copies, and over 75 percent may be sung unaccompanied. Such versatility allows the energetic congregation to find and claim its voice in a way that will serve them for generations to come. A community taking this music to heart will be a manifestation of the careful craft of the poet and composer. The harvest of song will indeed have come from "a field of voices raised up and gathered."

Marilyn Haskel
Consulting Editor for Music
Church Publishing

Foreword

When you open the pages of this book of 30 hymns, you are likely to find something that expresses the longings and desires of your soul this day. From joy to sorrow, from closeness to abandonment, from wholeness to pain, from God to individual, the human experience is well-traversed.

Words are simple and extremely well-crafted. Their simplicity allows space for all the layers of meaning that experience brings to a hymn text. While they are new words, I suspect they will be durable over the years.

The tunes and harmonies are also simple and extremely well-crafted. They "sing" well, they explore the richness of human emotion, and they command the attentiveness of the singer. They call forth both spiritual and vocal energies in ways that will be, at the same time, demanding and rewarding.

It should be no surprise that David and Jim have made such a collection. Each knows his craft very well, each has had a wide variety of life experiences, each knows the art of the other well, each knows and cares deeply for the body of Christ, and they are friends. I would hope all of you who read and sing from the pages of this book will be blessed by this visitation to the life of your soul from this pair of brothers in Christ.

Ken Nafziger
Professor of Music
Eastern Mennonite University
Harrisonburg, Virginia

Introduction: Hymns for the Body

Often, when someone asks about our work together, they want to know which comes first, music or words? The answer, frankly, is neither.

Instead, what generates our work is a combination of our own spiritual needs and the felt needs of the communities to which we belong. We're interested in collaborating not merely with one another; we want to make an integral connection with the people who will encounter our music. In fact, we would argue that music, especially music written for congregational use, is incomplete until it finds its way into the bodies of others—whether they hear it, perform it, or sing it together in worship. So we offer these hymns for worship, hoping that a wide variety of believers will help us to complete them, again and again.

Written over the course of two years, the hymns in this collection have grown from the ground of an unexpected friendship. In the fall of 2001, we met at Lombard Mennonite Church where Jim, for a number of years, had accompanied and written music for worship, and where his wife, Angie, served as choral conductor and song leader. Our families became part of the same fellowship group, and Dave became involved over time in the church choir.

The two of us also began to meet regularly on Sunday mornings, skipping Sunday school to drink coffee and talk about music, Wendell Berry's poetry, and Monty Python films. To our delight, no one ever criticized this delinquent behavior, recognizing, perhaps, that these quirky and spirited conversations were necessary, at least for us.

We are quite different in some ways. Jim is fairly private and devoted to detail while Dave is avidly social and prone to grand ideas. But we share in common a powerful connection: a lifelong experience of language and song as primary means of God's presence in our lives. Initially, this connection resulted in collaborations on choral music for adults and children, and in a song cycle about being parents. Eventually, we turned our attention to hymns for worship. Our first collaborative hymn—"Jesus, offered up as bread"—came quickly (if we don't consider the two years of conversation leading up to it) and was warmly received by our faith community. Neither of us realized at the time the luxury of worshiping in the same church or being able to meet for lunch on the Wheaton College campus or at the Clemens home. We simply enjoyed the freedom of writing music together and immediately experiencing these songs as part of corporate worship.

While we might not have articulated it then, we realize now that we were sharpening our conviction that music needs others, beyond the collaboration between poet and composer. For a score to be a song, it requires the generous presence of musicians, listeners, and worshipers who allow music into their minds, give it life with their breath, shape the words on their tongues and then hear them resonate in their ears and chest. And in Christian worship, when we are alert and open enough, the Holy Spirit joins and enlivens this singing.

Later in 2004, when we both moved away from the Chicago suburbs—the Wright family to Central Illinois and the Clemens family to Virginia's Shenandoah Valley—we set up new challenges for ourselves. How could we maintain friendship and creative energy via phone and email? How might we write music for worship while attending very different churches? How should we extend what we were learning as artists and as believers and move beyond what we'd grown comfortable writing? How do we find God's leading in a new place?

The answers to those questions are, for now, contained in these hymns. We discovered that our new environments stimulated new kinds of texts and tunes. We found that at a distance we could write one or two hymns over a long period of time. Then, when we got together for a week in Michigan at Camp Friedenswald and later at Jim's home in Virginia, we experienced an enormous burst of creative energy, resulting in many pieces taking shape in quick succession. We also learned that in either situation numerous false starts and the appearance of "shadow hymns" with questionable and/or silly lyrics seem to be essential parts of our composition process (and a hidden part of the process that should, and will, remain in the shadows).

In each writing situation, we enjoy challenging and questioning one another. Dave occasionally suggests a melodic line or harmonic texture while Jim insists that syllables land in the right places so that each word works not only for the sake of image or meaning but also for sound. Sometimes, we even overlap in our artistic roles, with Jim composing words or Dave writing a tune. We have relied regularly on the responses of trusted mentors, worship leaders, pastors, and writers who have made pointed, generous suggestions that we work to incorporate as we revise.

This collection includes the fruit of these suggestions and of our give and take. The notes we've compiled provide ideas on how particular hymns might be incorporated into worship. We hope these suggestions, the indexes, and the brief services will be the genesis of creativity for those who engage this music. We also hope musicians and congregations will let us know of the ideas that arise in their own encounters with these songs.

Ultimately, the process of making these hymns has built up both our friendship and our faith. We have enjoyed our struggle together to combine biblically resonant language with musical structures that can be sung by God's people in community. In other words, we have attempted to make hymns that diverse individuals can embody and sing with integrity, music that can be sung by the whole body of Christ, "a field of voices, raised up and gathered."

True worship, Kathleen Norris reminds us, "resists and transcends overt attempts at manipulation . . . . Worship requires people with open ears and hearts. At its root, the word 'liturgy' simply means 'the work of the people.'" And so the success of any hymn depends on God's grace and on the grace of those who faithfully offer up this music, or any other, as their own, as a "harvest of song."

Jim Clemens
David Wright
Advent 2006

As we rise, O God, to meet you

SPIRIT, FILL US 87. 87 with refrain

I
All I 1 As we rise, O God, to meet you,
Women & Children I, Men II 2 As we gath - er, God, to - geth - er,
Men I, Women & Children II 3 As we lin - ger at your ta - ble,
Women & Children I, Men II 4 As we learn, O God, to love you,
All I 5 As we go, O God, to serve you,
II
1 as we o - pen wide our eyes, like the sun that
2 as each tongue here learns to sing, like the birds that
3 as we eat this com - mon bread, like the seed both
4 as we lis - ten for your voice, like the dust from
5 as we o - pen wide our hands, like the wind that
1 fills the morn - ing, fill our bod - ies with your light.
2 fill the for - ests, fill our bod - ies with your song.
3 sown and scat - tered, fill our bod - ies with new life.
4 which you made us, fill our bod - ies with your breath.
5 moves the wa - ters, spread your peace to ev - ery land.
Refrain (All)
We are emp-ty. Spir - it, fill us. God, we o - pen up our
lives.

Text: David Wright, 2005

Music: James E. Clemens, 2005

For piano part, see Accompaniments.

Blessed

BEATITUDES 85. 85. 65. 85

1 Bless - ed, bless - ed, loved and bless - ed,
2 Bless - ed, bless - ed, loved and bless - ed,
3 Bless - ed, bless - ed, loved and bless - ed,
4 Bless - ed, bless - ed, loved and bless - ed, your

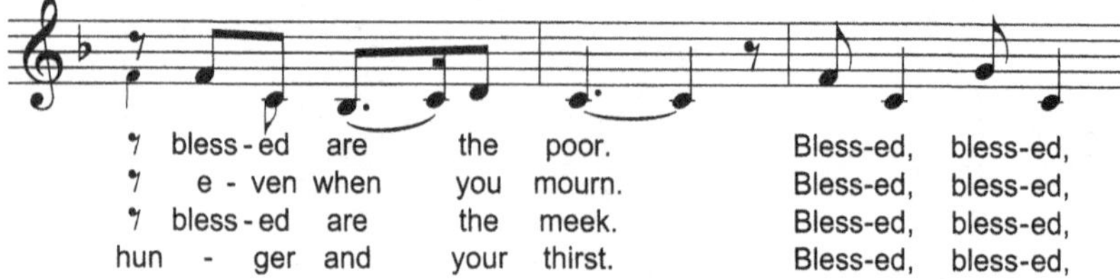
bless - ed are the poor. Bless-ed, bless-ed,
e - ven when you mourn. Bless-ed, bless-ed,
bless - ed are the meek. Bless-ed, bless-ed,
hun - ger and your thirst. Bless-ed, bless-ed,

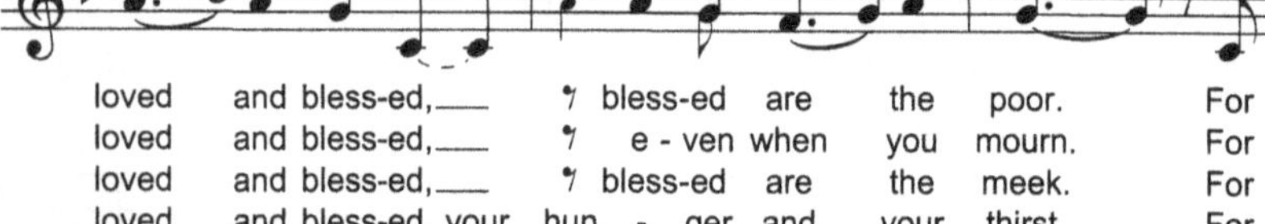
loved and bless-ed, bless-ed are the poor. For
loved and bless-ed, e - ven when you mourn. For
loved and bless-ed, bless-ed are the meek. For
loved and bless-ed, your hun - ger and your thirst. For

theirs is the king - dom, theirs is the
you shall find com - fort, you shall find
theirs is cre - a - tion, theirs is cre -
you shall be filled, you shall be

king - dom. Bless-ed, bless-ed, loved and bless-ed,
com - fort. Bless-ed, bless-ed, loved and bless-ed,
a - tion. Bless-ed, bless-ed, loved and bless-ed,
filled. Bless-ed, bless-ed, loved and bless-ed, your

Text: David Wright, 2005

Music: David Wright and James E. Clemens

For piano part, see Accompaniments.

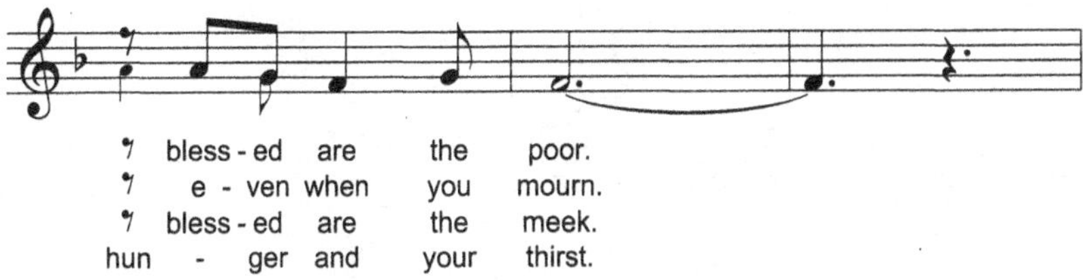
bless - ed are the poor.
e - ven when you mourn.
bless - ed are the meek.
hun - ger and your thirst.

5 Blessed, blessed, loved and blessed, when mercy fills your heart. (2x)
For you will know mercy, you will know mercy.
Blessed, blessed, loved and blessed, when mercy fills your heart.

6 Blessed, blessed, loved and blessed, when your heart is pure. (2x)
For you will see God, you will see God.
Blessed, blessed, loved and blessed, when your heart is pure. .

7 Blessed, blessed, loved and blessed, those who bring God's peace. (2x)
For you are God's children, you are God's children.
Blessed, blessed, loved and blessed, those who bring God's peace.

8 Blessed, blessed, loved and blessed, even when you're scorned. (2x)
For yours is the kingdom, yours is the kingdom.
Blessed, blessed, loved and blessed, even when you're scorned.

Breath in the wind

PRESENCE 458. 459

1,5 Breath in the wind, voice in the wa - ter,
2 Thun - der - ing clouds, shel - ter - ing wood - land,
3 Heat of the day, cool of the eve - ning,
4 Broad as the plains, full as the vil - lage,
arm as strong as the moun - tain high.
word that rides on the whis - pered air.
shad - ow long in the set - ting sun.
heart and pulse of the bound - less land.
Breath in the wind, voice in the wa - ter,
Thun - der - ing clouds, shel - ter - ing wood - land,
Heat of the day, cool of the eve - ning,
Broad as the plains, full as the vil - lage,
love fall - ing free like rain from the sky.
hope as deep as the lake so clear.
peace stretch-ing far as the des - ert sand.
grace as near as a neigh - bor's hand.

Text: David Wright

Music: James E. Clemens

By the river, by the stream
LAURELVILLE 85. 96 with refrain
Refrain
By the riv-er, by the stream, where we sing and weep,
by the riv - er of your love, O Sav - ior, plant us deep.
Fine
Leader
1 How can we sing a song of joy,
2 How can we sing a song of hope,
3 How can we sing a song of peace,
All
where we sing and
a song of joy in a for - eign land?
a song of hope in a dis - tant land?
a song of peace in a vi - o - lent land?
weep,
O
To refrain
Oh,
To refrain
Sav - ior, plant us deep.

Text: David Wright, 2006, based on Psalm 137

Music: James E. Clemens, 2006

Christ be with me

BLESSING LMD

1 Christ be with me, Christ with - in me,
2 Christ be - neath me, Christ a - bove me,
Christ be - hind me, Christ be - fore me,
Christ in qui - et, Christ in dan - ger,
Christ be - side me, Christ to win me,
Christ in hearts of all that love me,
Christ to com - fort and re - store me.
Christ in mouth of friend and strang - er.

Text: attributed to St. Patrick, *Irish Liber Hymnorum*, 1897; tr. Cecil F. Alexander, 1889, *Writings of St. Patrick*, 1889
Music: James E. Clemens, 2005

Come make a noise

JOYFUL SONG 12 10. 12 10

1 Come make a noise to the Lord, the God of heav - en.
2 Wor - ship the Lord with re - joic - ing and thanks - giv - ing.

1 Come make a noise to God.
2 Wor - ship the Lord; re - joice.

Come make a noise, O make a joy - ful song. Come make a noise
Wor - ship the Lord, lift up a joy - ful song. Wor - ship the Lord

Come make a noise, a joy - ful song. Come make a noise
Wor - ship the Lord with joy - ful song. Wor - ship the Lord;

to the Lord, the God of heav - en. All of the earth will sing a
with re - joic - ing and thanks - giv - ing. All of the earth will sing a

to God. All of the earth
re - joice. All of the earth

joy - ful song.
joy - ful song.

will sing. All of the earth will sing a joy - ful song.
will sing. All of the earth will sing a joy - ful song.

Text: David Wright, based on Psalm 100

Music: James E. Clemens

Come to the table

COME TO THE TABLE 9 9 8

2
1 Come, come,
2 Come, come,
3 Come, come,
For sending: Go, go,

come to the ta - ble in love. We
come to the ta - ble in need. We
come to the ta - ble in truth. We
go from the ta - ble in peace. We

come to - geth - er in Je - sus' name. We
come to - geth - er in Je - sus' name. We
come to - geth - er in Je - sus' name. We
go to live___ in Je - sus' name. We

come to the ta - ble in love.
come to the ta - ble in need.
come to the ta - ble in truth.
go from the ta - ble in peace.

Additional verses:

4 Come … in hope.
5 Come … with thanks.
6 Come … in song.
7 Come … with friends.
8 Come … and eat.

Text: James E. Clemens, 2006
Music: James E. Clemens, 2006

For piano part, see Accompaniments.

Come! Walk in the light

Refrain

COME! WALK IN THE LIGHT Irregular with refrain

Come! Walk in the light. Come! walk in the light of day.
Come! Walk in the light. Come! walk in the light of day.

For piano part, see Accompaniments.

1 In the days ahead, the nations will stream to the house of the Holy One.
Many peoples will turn to God. They will learn God's ways and walk in God's light.

2 And God will judge every nation and tribe. They will beat their swords into plows,
and their spears into pruning hooks. Never shall they practice war anymore.

3 The wolf and the lamb will live together. The cattle will graze with the bear;
their young will lie down together. On God's holy mountain will there be peace.

4 Let the mountains be laden with God's peace, and the hills be filled with justice.
Like showers that water the earth, let God's light rain on the valleys and fields.

5 O God, Lord of Hosts, how long? How long, O Lord, will you be angry with our prayers,
will you feed us the bread of our tears? Restore us. Let us walk again in your light.

6 Lift your eyes. Arise. Shine. Your light has come. Now you will see and be radiant.
The brightness of the dawn is here. God makes the way clear. Come, walk in the light.

Alternate Refrain (unaccompanied)

Come! Walk in the light. Come! Walk in the light of day.
Come! Walk, walk in the light. Walk in the light of day.
Come! Walk, walk in the light. Walk in the light, the light of day.
Come! Walk in the light. Come! Walk in the light of day.
Come! Walk, walk in the light. Walk in the light of day.
Come! Walk, walk in the light. Walk in the light, the light of day.

Text: Advent 2004 Committee (refrain), 2003; David Wright (verses), 2005

Music: James E. Clemens, 2003, 2005

Come, brother, sit with me

HOSPITALITY 66. 66. 10 6

1 Come, broth - er, sit with me, shar - ing this sim - ple bread.
2 Come, stran - ger, walk with me, shar - ing the nar - row road.
3 Go, chil - dren, sing with joy, prais - ing the ris - en Lord.
Optional Part II
1 Come, sit with me, share this
2 Come, walk with me, share the
3 Go, sing with joy, praise the
Come, sis - ter, to my home, drink till you've had your fill.
Come, wise one, talk with me, show me the bet - ter way.
Go, ser - vants, to the world, borne on the Spir - it's strength.
bread. Come to my home, drink your
road. Come, talk with me, show the
Lord. Go, to the world, borne on
Who gives these gifts of friend - ship and ta - ble?
Who gives these gifts of wis - dom and won - der?
Who gives these gifts of wor - ship and ser - vice?
fill. Who gives friend - ship and
way. Who gives wis - dom and
strength. Who gives wor - ship and

Text: David Wright, 2006

Music: James E. Clemens, 2006

1, 2
None but the liv - ing God.
ta - ble?
won - der? None but the liv - ing God.
ser - vice?
3
God, the liv-ing God, liv-ing God.
but the liv-ing God, the liv-ing God.

Gloria in excelsis Deo!

GLORIA Irregular

Leader
All
Glo-ri-a in ex-cel - sis De - o! Glo-ri-a in ex-cel - sis De - o!
Leader
All
Glo - ry to God in the high-est! Glo - ry to God in the high - est!
Al - le - lu - ia!

Music: James E. Clemens, 2005

Go, my friends, in grace

BENEDICTUS DEUS 56. 66
1 Go, my friends, in grace, be - neath the
2 Walk, my friends, in peace, with - in this
3 Serve, my friends, in love, your neigh - bors
4 Come a - gain, my friends, to wor - ship
1 bless - ed sky. Where you go, God is
2 fall - en world. Where you walk, God is
3 and your foes. Where you serve, God is
4 and to pray. When we meet, God is
1-3
1 there, be - neath the bless - ed sky.
2 there, with - in this fall - en world.
3 there, in neigh - bors and in foes.
4
4 here. Ben-e - dic - tus De - us.*

*Translation: Blessed be God

Text: David Wright, 2004

Music: James E. Clemens, 2004

God hears our cries

GOD HEARS Irregular

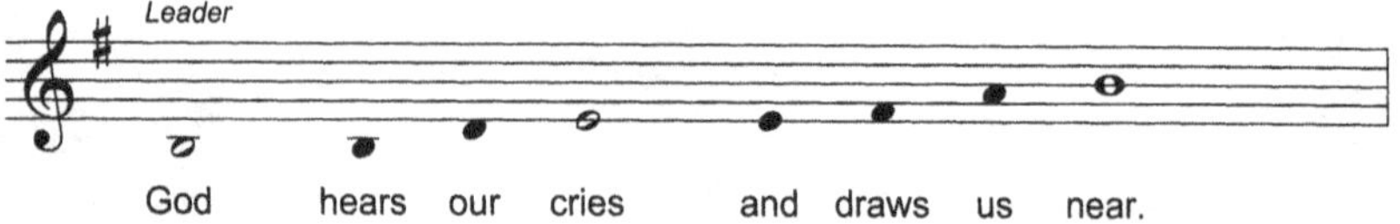
Leader
God hears our cries and draws us near.

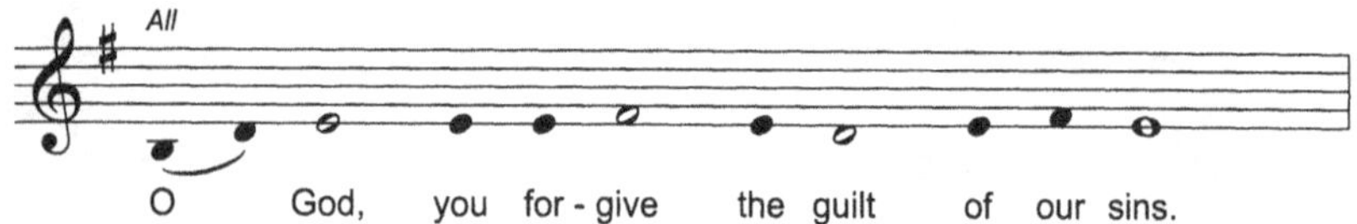
All
O God, you for - give the guilt of our sins.

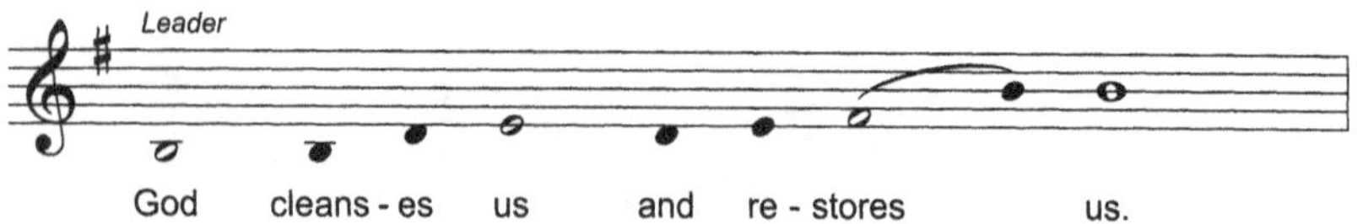
Leader
God cleans - es us and re - stores us.

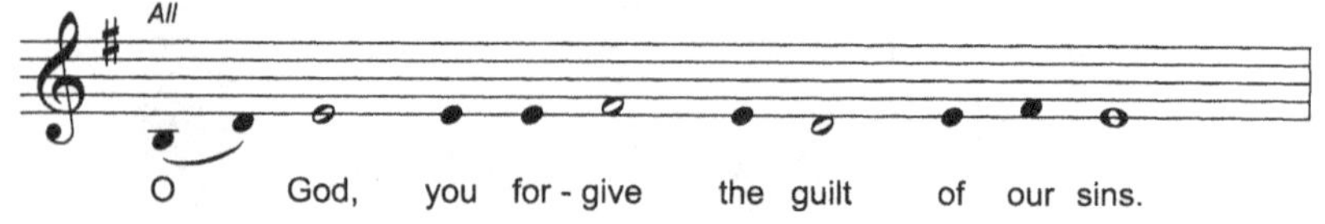
All
O God, you for - give the guilt of our sins.

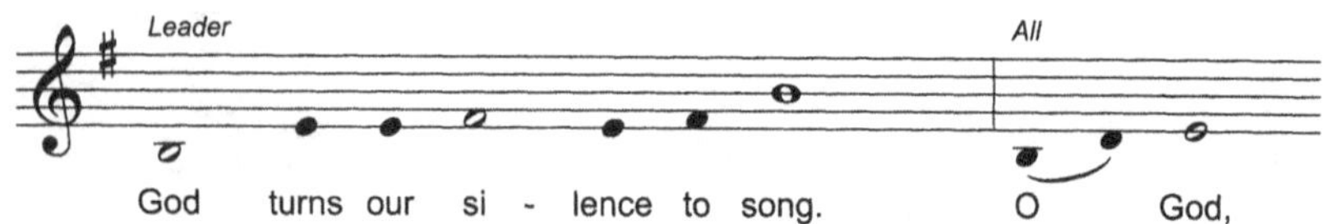
Leader
God turns our si - lence to song.
All
O God,

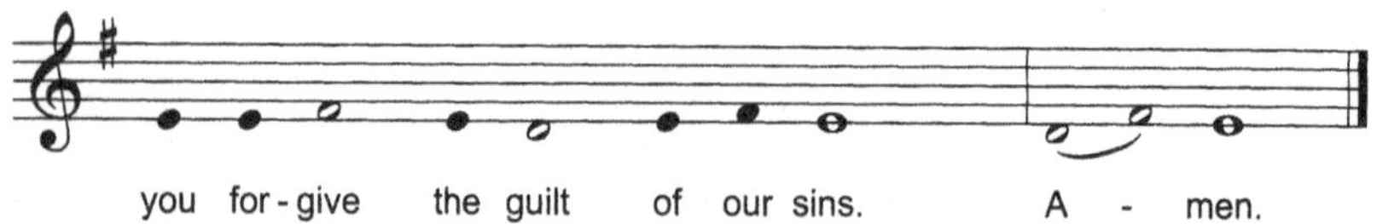
you for - give the guilt of our sins. A - men.

Text: David Wright, 2005, based on Psalm 32:5

Music: James E. Clemens, 2005

God who has saved

SURROUND US WITH SONG 99. 96
Canon*
God who has saved, sur - round us with song, sur -
round us with hymns of sal - va - tion.
God who has saved, sur - round us with song,
turn our si - lence to prais - es.

*Two, three, or four parts, at the measure or half measure

Text: David Wright, based on Psalm 32:7

Music: James E. Clemens

Here in this body

BOUND TOGETHER 546. 448

2
All, unison
1 Here in this bod - y,
2 Here in this bod - y,
3 Here in this bod y,
4 Here in this bod - y,

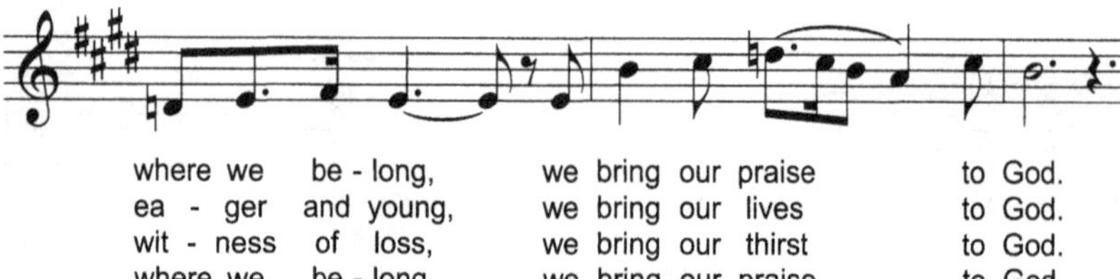
where we be - long, we bring our praise to God.
ea - ger and young, we bring our lives to God.
wit - ness of loss, we bring our thirst to God.
where we be - long, we bring our praise to God.

Harmony
S.A.
Head, heart, and hands, mus - cle and bone,
Vig - or and strength pas - sion and fear,
Hands that are cupped, fill them with hope.
Head, heart, and hands, mus - cle and bone,
T.B.

bound to - geth - er in praise, we sing. Here in this
bound to - geth - er in hope, we sing. Here in this
Bound to - geth - er by truth we sing. Here in this
bound to - geth - er in praise we sing. When in this

Text: David Wright, 2006

Music: James E. Clemens, 2006

For piano part, see Accompaniments.

bod - y, im - age of God, we
bod - y, bro - ken by sin, we
bod - y, worn by the years, we
bod - y, ris - en and new, we
bring our - selves to God. Wom - en and
bring our cries to God. Wound - ed and
bring our past to God. Dust in - to
know God's end - less song. Heav - en and
men, formed from the dust, bound to-
bruised, mend - ed and whole, bound to-
dust, yearn - ing for rest. Bound to-
earth, made new in Christ. Bound to-
Wom - en and men, formed from the dust, bound to-
Wound - ed and bruised, mend - ed and whole, bound to-
Dust in - to dust, yearn - ing for rest. Bound to-
Heav - en and earth, made new in Christ. Bound to-
geth - er by love, we sing.
geth - er by grace, we sing.
geth - er by peace, we sing.
geth - er in joy, we'll sing.

Jesus, offered up as bread

TABLE ROUND 77. 85

Dm G Dm

1 Je - sus, of - fered up as bread,
2 Je - sus, of - fered up as wine,
3 Je - sus, mak - er of this feast,

Dm/F Am G Dm

Je - sus, on this ta - ble spread,
Je - sus, from the heav - y vine,
Je - sus, lov - er of the least,

G Dm

In our emp - ty hands we take you,
On our thirst - ing tongues we take you,
At your ta - ble, no one hun - gers;

Dm/F Am Gsus G Dm

bro - ken as the bread.
poured out as the wine.
let us keep your feast.

(This can be sung as a two-part canon, unaccompanied, with group 2 beginning eight measures after group 1.)

Version 2

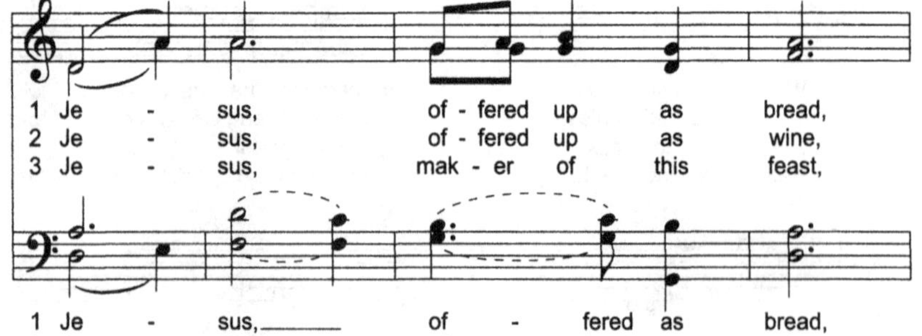
1 Je - sus, of - fered up as bread,
2 Je - sus, of - fered up as wine,
3 Je - sus, mak - er of this feast,
1 Je - sus, of - fered as bread,
2 Je - sus, of - fered as wine,
3 Je - sus, you made this feast,

Text: David Wright, 2004

Music: James E. Clemens, 2004

Je - sus, on this ta - ble spread,
Je - sus, from the heav - y vine,
Je - sus, lov - er of the least,
Je - sus, the ta - ble spread,
Je - sus, the heav - y vine,
Je - sus, you love the least;
In our emp - ty hands we take you,
On our thirst - ing tongues we take you,
At your ta - ble, no one hun - gers;
In our emp - ty hands we take you,
On our thirst - ing tongues we take you,
At your ta - ble, no one hun - gers;
1, 2
bro - ken as the bread.
poured out as the wine.
let us keep your
bro - ken as the bread.
poured out as the wine.
let us keep your
3
feast. A - men.
feast. A - men.

Jesus calls us

FOLLOW Irregular

Leader
All
1,5 Je - sus calls us:
2 "Bring your bur - dens."
3 "Rise and walk now."
4 "Seek the king - dom."
"Come fol - low me.
Come fol - low, fol - low, fol - low, come fol - low me."
Fol - low, fol - low,
Leader
All
Je - sus calls us:
"Bring your bur - dens."
"Rise and fol - low."
"Seek the king - dom."
"Come fol - low me.
Come fol - low, fol - low, fol - low, fol - low me."
Fol - low, fol - low,

Text: James E. Clemens and David Wright, 2006

Music: James E. Clemens, 2006

Kyrie eleison

HEAR OUR PRAYER 644

1 Ky - ri - e e - lei - son. Lord, have
2 Chris - te e - lei - son. Christ, have
3 Ky - ri - e e - lei - son. Lord, have
mer - cy; Lord, hear our prayer.
mer - cy; Christ, hear our prayer.
mer - cy; grant us your peace.

Text: James E. Clemens, 2005
Music: James E. Clemens, 2005

O God, be gracious

SHINE UPON US Irregular

Canon
1
O God, be gra - cious to us and bless us;
make your face shine up - on us, that your
2
way may be known up - on the earth, your
sav - ing pow'r a - mong the na - tions.
3
Let the peo - ples praise you; let
all the peo - ples praise you.

Text: James E Clemens, 2006, paraphrase of Psalm 67:1–3
Music: James E. Clemens, 2006

Oh, Abram, look up to the sky

LOOK UP TO THE SKY 65. 65 with refrain
Leader
1 Oh, A - bram, oh, A - bram,
3 Oh, A - bra - ham, oh, A - bra-ham,
All
look up to the sky.
take up your new name.
Leader
Oh, A - bram,
Oh, A - bra-ham,
oh, A - bram,
oh, A - bra-ham,
All
look up to the sky.
take up your new name.
To refrain
Refrain
All
See the stars as man - y as the sands.
Look up to the sky. See your chil - dren, all your chil - dren. Look up to the sky.
Fine
Leader
2 Oh, Sa - rai, oh, Sa - rai,
4 Oh, Sa - rah, oh, Sa - rah,
All
laugh - ing at the sky.
take up your new name.
Leader
Oh, Sa - rai,
Oh, Sa - rah,
oh, Sa - rai,
oh, Sa - rah,
All
laugh - ing at the sky.
take up your new name.
To refrain

Text: David Wright, 2004

Music: James E. Clemens, 2005

Oh, sister, I beg you to listen to me

EXPRESSION 11 11. 9 11

Unison
1 Oh, sis - ter, I beg you to lis - ten to me, so
2 Oh, broth - er, I beg you to lis - ten to me, so
3 Oh, Je - sus, I beg you to lis - ten to me, so
far from the Sav - ior, so far from your home.
far from the Sav - ior, so far from your home.
far from you, Sav - ior, so far from my home.
Harmony
Come home, come home, wher - ev - er you've
Come home, come home, wher - ev - er you've
Come home, come home, oh, I long to come
been. Come home to the Sav - ior who calls you by name.
been. Come home to the Sav - ior who calls you by name.
home, come home to the Sav - ior who calls me by name.

Text: David Wright, 2005

Music: Anonymous, *The Sacred Harp*, 1844; arranged by James E. Clemens, 2006

Open my ears, open my eyes

INVOCATION Irregular

4
Ears,
eyes,
hands,
4
arms,
mind,
heart—
Come, Je - sus,
come.
Ears
and
eyes,
hands
and
arms,
mind
and
heart—
O
come, Je - sus,
come.
My ears,
my eyes,
my

Text: James E. Clemens, 2005
Music: James E. Clemens, 2005

For piano part, see Accompaniments.

hands, my arms, my mind, my heart—
Come, Je-sus, come. My ears, my eyes, my
hands, my arms, my mind, my heart— O
come, Je-sus, come. O-pen my ears, o-pen my
eyes, o-pen my hands, o-pen my arms, o-pen my

mind, o-pen my heart— O come, Je - sus,
come. O-pen my ears, o-pen my eyes, o-pen my
hands, o-pen my arms, o-pen my mind, o-pen my
heart— O come, Je - sus, come. o-pen my
mind, o-pen my heart— O come, Je - sus, come.

Pass this bread to your brother

GIFT OF LIFE 75. 75. 65

1 Pass this bread to your broth - er, take it in your hand. Pass this bread to your sis - ter, take it in your hand. Taste the bread, gift of life from the hand of God.
2 Pass this cup to your broth - er, take it in your hand. Pass this cup to your sis - ter, take it in your hand. Drink the cup, gift of life from the hand of God.
3 Eat this meal with your broth - ers, eat it with your friends. Eat this meal with your sis - ters, eat it with your friends. Taste and see, gift of life from the hand of God.

Text: David Wright, 2004

Music: David Wright and James E. Clemens, 2004

Restore us

RESTORE US Irregular

Leader
All
Re-store us, O God. Re-store us, O God. Lead us in-to your pres-ence.

Text: James E. Clemens, 2006
Music: James E. Clemens, 2006

Seek the peace of the city

SEEK THE PEACE 75. 85

1 Seek the peace of the cit - y; make this land your home. I have set you here to pros - per; make this land your home.
2 Seek the peace of your neigh - bor, en - e - my or friend. I can break the hard - est heart, en - e - my or friend.
3 Seek the peace of the ex - ile, strang - er on the road. I will walk a - long be - side you, strang - er on the road.
4 Seek the peace of the Sav - ior; I will draw you near. I will bring you home for - ev - er; I will draw you near.
5 Seek the peace of the cit - y; find me in this place. I have brought you here to know me; find me in this place.
1-4
5

Text: David Wright, 2004, based on Jeremiah 29:7

Music: James E. Clemens, 2004

Set your troubled hearts at rest

RESTING HEARTS 77. 85

1 Set your trou - bled hearts at rest, set your trou - bled
hearts at rest, trou - bled
2 Lay your heav - y bur - dens down, lay your heav - y
bur - dens down, heav - y
3 Trust me in your un - be - lief, trust me in your
un - be - lief, in your
4 Set your trou - bled hearts at rest, set your trou - bled
hearts at rest, trou - bled
1 hearts at rest. I have stilled the wild - est thun - der;
2 bur - dens down. I have come to be your broth - er;
3 un - be - lief. I have met you in your doubt - ing;
4 hearts at rest. I have made a dwell - ing for you;
I will give you rest. (give you rest.)
lay your bur - dens down. (bur - dens down.)
trust me and be - lieve. (and be - lieve.)
I will give you rest. (give you rest.)

Text: David Wright, 2004, based on John 14:1–7
Music: James E. Clemens, 2004

Sing to the Lord of the harvest

HARVEST 87. 10 7 with refrain

1 Sing to the Lord of the har - vest,
2 Sing to the Lord of the har - vest,
3 Give to the Lord of the har - vest the
4 Come to the Lord of the har - vest.
mak - er of field and of sky. God of the sea-sons both
giv - er of days and of years. God of the fu - ture, the
work and the joy of our hands. God of the na-tions, and
Come to the ta - ble; re - joice! God, who has giv - en the
fal - low and full, speak - ing the world in - to life.
pres-ent, the past, through and be - yond all our fears.
au - thor of peace, teach us your grace - ful com - mands.
hun - ger for song, fill us with breath and with voice.

Text: David Wright

Music: James E. Clemens

Refrain
A field of voic - es raised up and gath - ered,
A field of voic - es gath - ered, we
now we of - fer a har - vest of song. Hear our hal - le-
of - fer a har - vest of song.
lu - jah. Hear our grate - ful a - men.

The smallest things

4
1 See how the grass of the
4
(2nd time only)
field stands tall; see how it grac - es the
mead - ow: Ev - 'ry blade that
God has made, a taste of Cre -
a - tion's glo - ry. ry.
1
2

Text: David Wright, 2005, based on Matthew 6:25–34
Music: James E. Clemens, 2005

For piano part, see Accompaniments.

Refrain
Sing hal - le - lu - jah for the small - est
things, the grass of the field, the birds of the
air. Sing hal - le - lu - jah for the
Last time to Coda
small - est things, God's own
(Sing refrain twice after v. 2)
hand is ev - 'ry - where.

4
(2nd time only)
2 Look, look
4
2 Look at the flow'r and
what the flow - er wears; look,
what it wears, the fin - est
fin - est silk so yel - low.
silk so yel - low.
Look: ev - 'ry spring the
Ev - 'ry spring the hill - side
hill - side sings, in splen - did
sings, a choir in its splen - did

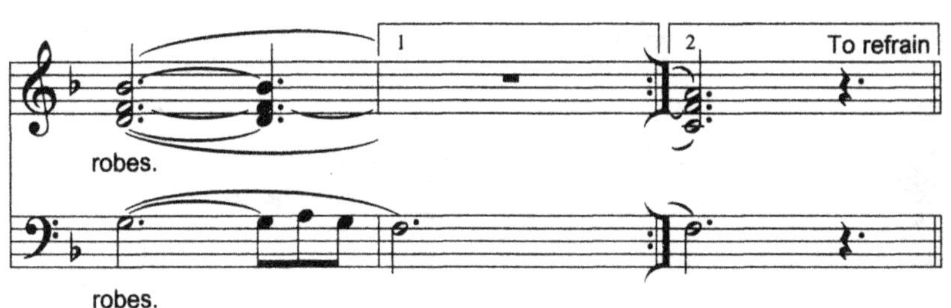
1
2
To refrain
robes.
robes.

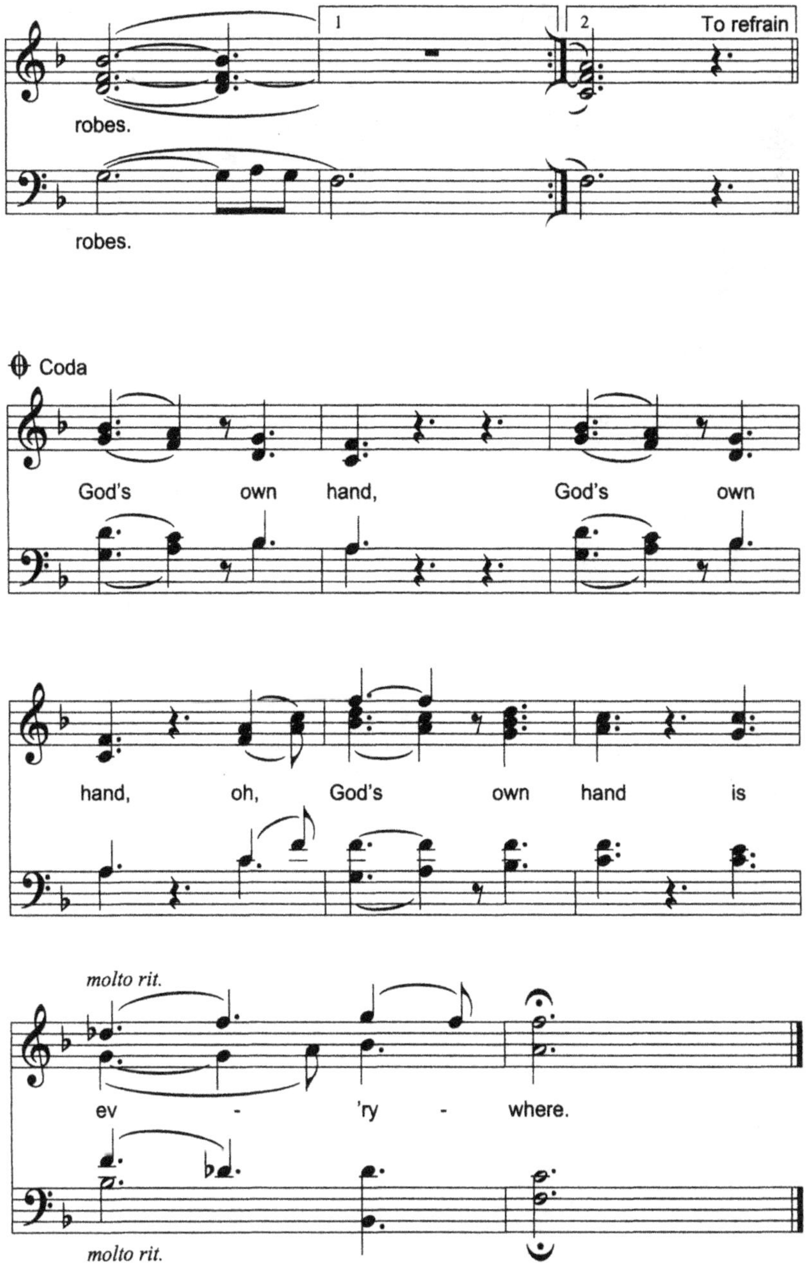

Coda

God's own hand, God's own

hand, oh, God's own hand is

molto rit.

ev - 'ry - where.

molto rit.

Turn to me and answer

TURN TO ME 64. 64

Canon
1
2
Turn to me and an-swer, O Lord my God.
Turn to me and an-swer, O Lord my God.

Text: James E. Clemens, 2006
Music: James E. Clemens, 2006

Wake us, Lord!

FRIEDENSWALD 67. 77. 66

Canon
1
2
Wake us, wake us, wake us! Wake us, wake us,
wake us, Lord! Give our hands good work to do.
Teach our tongues to sing your praise. To - day be-longs to
you. To - day be-longs to you.

Clapping/Percussion patterns (ad lib)

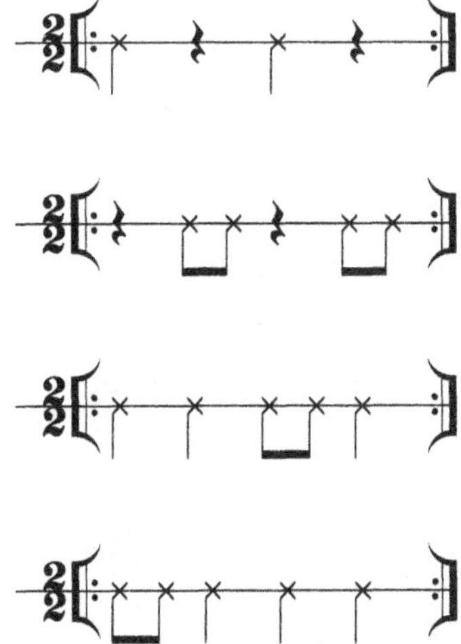

Text: David Wright, 2004

Music: James E. Clemens, 2004

While I keep silence

SILENCE 86. 86. 86
*
1 While I keep si - lence, si - lence,
2 My thirst - ing spir - it, spir - it,
3 All you who wan - der, wan - der,
si - lence in my flesh, my breath and bod - y
spir - it wastes a - way; I with - er in the
wan - der with - out hope, who know your man - y
*
fail. My sins grow bit - ter, bit - ter,
sun. But as I'm turn - ing, turn - ing,
sins, seek out the Sav - ior, Sav - ior,
bit - ter in my mouth. My bones re - turn to
turn - ing toward the night, you split the si - lent
Sav - ior while he's found; he hides you in his
*
dust. O God, I groan both day and
skies. O God, I stand be - neath the
hand. O God, you hear us day and
night, be - neath your heav - y hand.
rain, be - neath the cleans - ing rain.
night; re - store us by your hand.

*These notes may be hummed throughout the hymn, beginning at these places.

Accompaniments

ও

As we rise, O God, to meet you

SPIRIT, FILL US 87. 87 with refrain

D Am D Am7
I
1 As we rise, O God, to meet you, as we o - pen
2 As we gath - er, God, to - geth - er, as each tongue here
3 As we lin - ger at your ta - ble, as we eat this
4 As we learn, O God, to love you, as we lis - ten
5 As we go, O God, to serve you, as we o - pen
II
D Am7 D C D
1 wide our eyes, like the sun that fills the morn - ing,
2 learns to sing, like the birds that fill the for - ests,
3 com - mon bread, like the seed both sown and scat - tered,
4 for your voice, like the dust from which you made us,
5 wide our hands, like the wind that moves the wa - ters,
Am7 Gadd9 G D Am7 D

Text: David Wright, 2005

Music: James E. Clemens, 2005

For voice parts alone, see Hymns.

1 fill our bod - ies with your light.
2 fill our bod - ies with your song.
3 fill our bod - ies with new life.
4 fill our bod - ies with your breath.
5 spread your peace to ev - ery land.
C D Am7 D
Refrain (All)
We are emp - ty. Spir - it, fill us.
D2 Am7
God, we o - pen up our lives.
B♭add9 Cadd9 D Am
D Am7 (ties for ending only) D2

Blessed

BEATITUDES 85. 85. 65. 85

F Gm/F F Gm/F F Gm7 Csus Gm7/C
1 Bless-ed, bless-ed, loved and bless-ed, bless-ed are the
F Gm/F F Gm/F F Gm7
poor. Bless-ed, bless-ed, loved and bless-ed,
C no 3rd Gm7/C F Gm/F F Gm/F
bless-ed are the poor. For theirs is the
F Gm7 C no 3rd C B♭
Ped.
*

Text: David Wright, 2005

Music: David Wright and James E. Clemens

For all verses, see Hymns.

king - dom, theirs is the king - dom.
Am7/C Dm Gm Am7 B♭ Gm7/C
Bless-ed, bless-ed, loved and bless - ed, bless-ed are the
F Gm/F F Gm/F B♭maj7 Gm7/B♭
poor.
F Gm/F F Gm/F
F Gm7 Csus Gm7/C F

This page is left blank to facilitate page turns

Come to the table

COME TO THE TABLE 9 9 8

D D6add9 D D6add9 D D6add9 D D6add9
1 Come, come, come to the ta - ble in love. We come to - geth - er in Je - sus' name. We come to the ta - ble in love.
2 Come, come, come to the ta - ble in need. We come to - geth - er in Je - sus' name. We come to the ta - ble in need.
3 Come, come, come to the ta - ble in truth. We come to - geth - er in Je - sus' name. We come to the ta - ble in truth.
For sending: Go, go, go from the ta - ble in peace. We go to live in Je - sus' name. We go from the ta - ble in peace.
D D6add9 G G6add9 D Dadd9 D
Gadd9/B Dadd9/A G/A D D6add9 D D6add9 D2

Text: James E. Clemens, 2006
Music: James E. Clemens, 2006

For additional verses, see Hymns.

Come! Walk in the light

COME! WALK IN THE LIGHT

Refrain
Come! Walk in the light. Come! Walk in the light of day.
Capo 3: D Em7 F#m7 G D Em7 F Em7/A
F Gm7 Am7 B♭ F Gm7 A♭ Gm7/C

Fine
Come! Walk in the light. Come! Walk in the light of day.
D Em7 F#m7 Bm7 G Em7/A Dsus D
F Gm7 Am7 Dm7 B♭ Gm7/C Fsus F

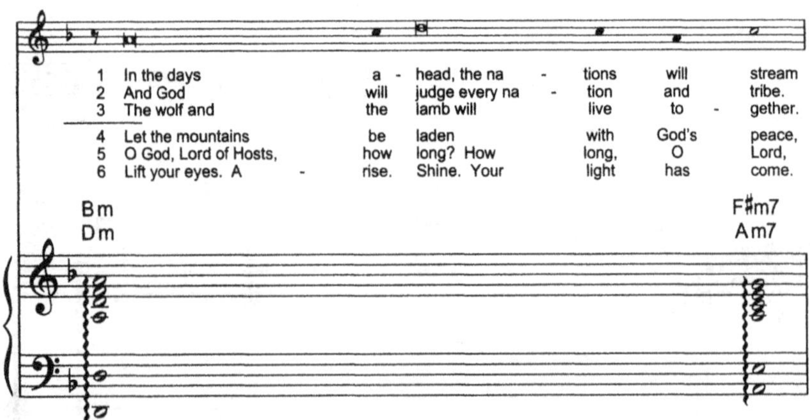
1 In the days a - head, the na - tions will stream
2 And God will judge every na - tion and tribe.
3 The wolf and the lamb will live to - gether.
4 Let the mountains be laden with God's peace,
5 O God, Lord of Hosts, how long? How long, O Lord,
6 Lift your eyes. A - rise. Shine. Your light has come.
Bm F#m7
Dm Am7

Text: Advent 2004 Committee (refrain), 2003; David Wright (verses), 2005

Music: James E. Clemens, 2003, 2005

For unaccompanied version, see Hymns.

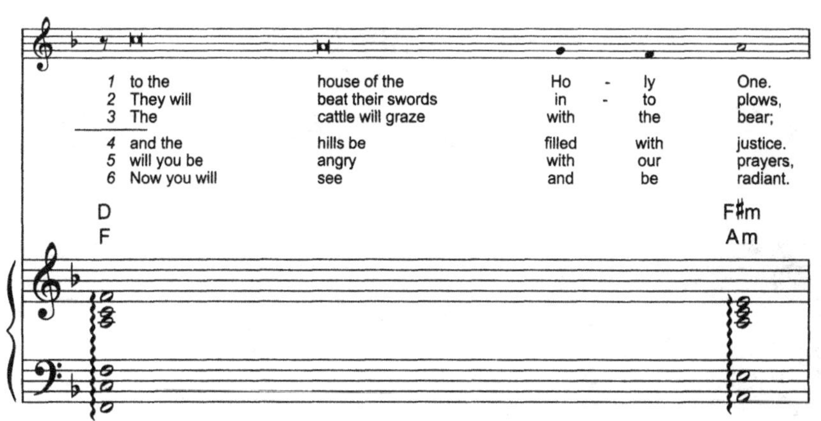
1 to the house of the Ho - ly One.
2 They will beat their swords in - to plows,
3 The cattle will graze with the bear;
4 and the hills be filled with justice.
5 will you be angry with our prayers,
6 Now you will see and be radiant.
D F F♯m Am

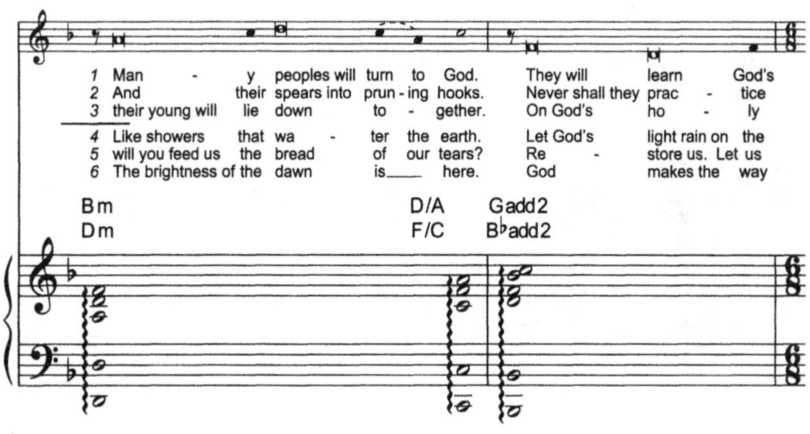
1 Man - y peoples will turn to God. They will learn God's
2 And their spears into prun - ing hooks. Never shall they prac - tice
3 their young will lie down to - gether. On God's ho - ly
4 Like showers that wa - ter the earth. Let God's light rain on the
5 will you feed us the bread of our tears? Re - store us. Let us
6 The brightness of the dawn is___ here. God makes the way
Bm Dm D/A F/C Gadd2 B♭add2

D.C.
1 ways and walk in God's light.
2 war___ an - y - more.
3 moun - tain will there be peace.
4 val - leys___ and fields.
5 walk a - gain in your light.
6 clear. Come, walk in the light.
Dadd2/F♯ Fadd2/A Gadd2/A B♭add2/C D/A F/C G/A B♭/C G6/A B♭6/C

Here in this body

BOUND TOGETHER 546. 448

1 Here in this bod - y,
E
E

where we be-long, we bring our praise to God.
D E Bm D A E

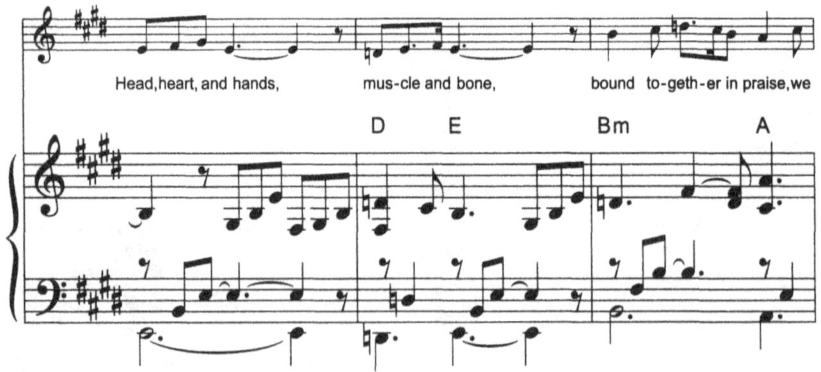
Head,heart, and hands, mus-cle and bone, bound to-geth-er in praise,we
D E Bm A

Text: David Wright, 2006

Music: James E. Clemens, 2006

For all verses, see Hymns.

sing. Here in this bod - y, im-age of God, we
E Bm Bm7 E
bring our - selves to God. Wom-en and men, formed from the
Bm Bm7 E G D
dust, bound to - geth-er by love, we sing.
E G D Bm7 E

Open my ears, open my eyes

INVOCATION Irregular

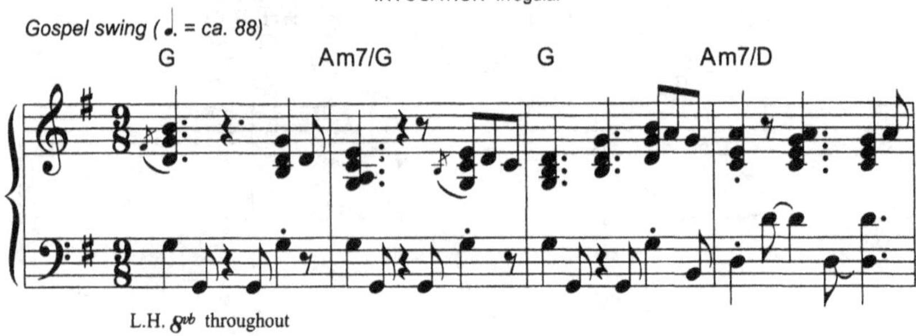
Gospel swing (♩. = ca. 88)
G
Am7/G
G
Am7/D
L.H. 8vb throughout

Ears,
eyes,
hands,
G
G7add9
C/G

arms,
mind,
heart—
Cm6/G
Cm6
Gmaj7
Bb7

Text: James E. Clemens, 2005
Music: James E. Clemens, 2005

For voice parts alone, see Hymns.

Come, Je - sus, come.
Ears and
eyes, hands and arms,
mind and heart—
O come, Je - sus,
Am7
Am7/D
D
G
A/B
B7
Cmaj7
A7
G/D
Am7/D
D6
E♭maj7
F7

come.
My ears,
my eyes,
my
Gadd2
Am7/D
G
G7add9
hands,
my arms,
my mind,
my
C/G
Cm6/G
Cm6
Gmaj7
heart—
Come, Je - sus,
come.
My
B♭7
Am7
Am7/D
D

ears, my eyes, my hands, my
G A/B B7 Cmaj7
arms, my mind, my heart— O
A7 G/D Am7/D D6
come, Je - sus, come. O-pen my
E♭maj7 F7 Gadd2 Am7/D

ears, o-pen my eyes, o-pen my hands, o-pen my
G G7add9 C/G
arms, o-pen my mind, o-pen my heart— O
Cm6/G Cm6 Gmaj7 B♭7
come, Je - sus, come. O-pen my ears, o-pen my eyes, o-pen my
Am7 Am7/D D7add9 G A/B B7

hands, o-pen my arms, o-pen my mind, o-pen my
Cmaj7
A7
G/D
heart— O come, Je - sus, come. o-pen my
Am7/D
D6
E♭maj7
F7
Gadd2
A7add9
rit.
mind, o-pen my heart— O come, Jesus, come.
rit.
G/D
Am7/D
D6
E♭maj7
F7
Gadd2
ad lib
rit.
(loco)

The smallest things

Gospel swing (♩. = ca. 88)
Gm F/A Gm/B♭ F/C C7 Gm7/F
L.H. 8vb throughout

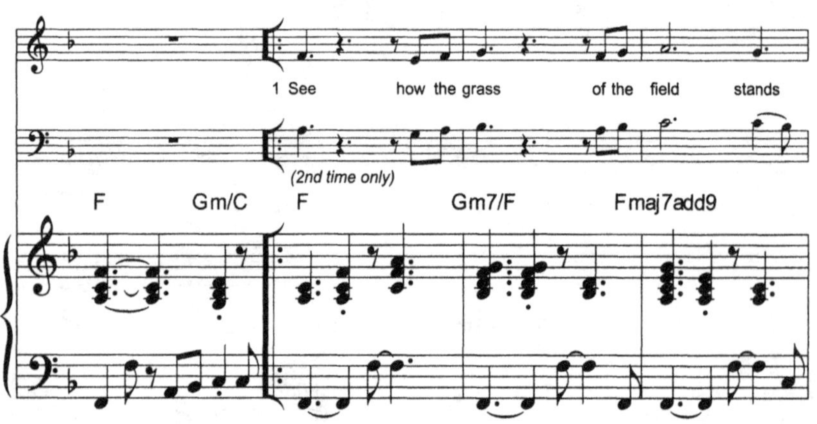
1 See how the grass of the field stands
(2nd time only)
F Gm/C F Gm7/F Fmaj7add9

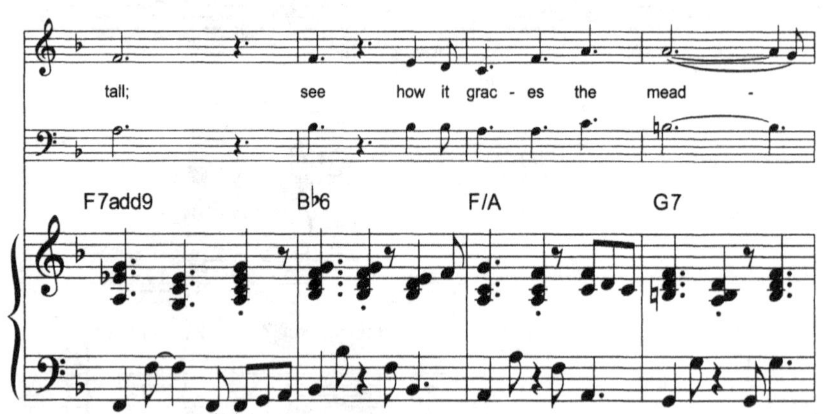
tall; see how it grac - es the mead -
F7add9 B♭6 F/A G7

Text: David Wright, 2005, based on Matthew 6:25–34
Music: James E. Clemens, 2005

For voice parts alone, see Hymns.

ow: Ev - 'ry blade that God has
Gm7/C C7 Fmaj7 Gm7 Am7sus Am7 A7♭9/C♯
made, a taste of Cre - a - tion's
Dm Gm6/D Dm7 Gm F/A Gm/B♭ F/C C
glo - ry. ry.
1 2
Gm7/F F Gm7/C F F7add9

Refrain
Sing hal - le - lu - jah for the small - est
B♭ B♭7add9 F A7 A7♯9 A7

things, the grass of the field, the
Dm F7/C B♭add2 F/A

birds of the air. Sing hal - le -
Gm7 Gm7/C C7 F7add9 B♭7add2

lu - jah for the small - est things,
F A7#5 A7 Dm A7sus/E D7/F♯

God's own hand is ev - 'ry - where.
Gm F/A Gm/B♭ F/C C7 B♭m6 F

Gm♭5 F/A B♭m6 F/A Gm7/C B♭m/F B♭m6/F

(2nd time only)
2 Look, look
2 Look at the flow'r and
F Gm7/C F Gm7/F
what the flow - er wears; look,
what it wears, the fin - est
Fmaj7add9 F7add2 E♭/F F7add9 B♭6
fin - est silk so yel - low.
silk so yel - low.
F/A G7 Gm7/C C7

Look: ev - 'ry spring the
Ev - 'ry spring the hill - side
Fmaj7
Gm7
Am7sus Am7 A7♭9/C♯
hill - side sings, in splen - did
sings, a choir in its splen - did
Dm Gm6/D Dm7
Gm F/A Gm/B♭
F/C C
robes.
robes.
Gm7/F
1
F Gm7/C
2
F E♭/F

Final refrain
Sing hal - le - lu - jah for the small - est
B♭ B♭7add9 F A7 A7♯9 A7
things, the grass of the field, the
Dm F7/C B♭add2 F/A
birds of the air. Sing hal - le -
Gm7 Gm7/C C7#5 F7add9 B♭7add2

lu - jah for the small - est things,
F
A7#5 A7
Dm A7sus/E D7/F♯
1
God's own hand is ev - 'ry -
1
Gm F/A Gm/B♭ F/C C7 B♭m6
where.
2
God's own hand,
F E♭/F
2
Gm F/A Gm/B♭ F/C

God's
own
hand,
oh,
God's
own
Gm
F/A
Gm/B♭
F/C
Gm
F/A
Gm/B
hand
is
ev
'ry
where.
molto rit.
molto rit.
F/C
C7
B♭m6
F
8va
molto rit.
Ped.

Notes

Introduction

Kathleen Norris' comment on worship comes from *Amazing Grace: A Vocabulary of Faith*. New York: Riverhead, 1998. 250.

As we rise, O God, to meet you

Inviting God's Spirit to enter our very bodies, this can be an invocation, a song of praise, a communion hymn, or part of a healing service. The final verse can also be used as a benediction. The song should be accompanied by piano, guitar, or both. It can also be helpful to have a tenor instrument, such as cello or viola, on the countermelody to support singers as they become comfortable with this part. Note the suggestions for trading the melody and countermelody between various groups of singers. These can be altered (for example, to include a choir or small ensemble). The idea, however, is to keep the vocal lines distributed evenly between voices and to rely on the accompaniment for harmonic textures. On the final time through, some song leaders may want to repeat the refrain. Because of the fairly complex figures of speech in each verse, the song should be taken at a tempo that allows for some reflection (having an ensemble sing a verse while the congregants listen can also assist in this regard).

Blessed

The beatitudes from the Sermon on the Mount (Matthew 5-7) and the Sermon on the Plain (Luke 6) form the core of the Mennonite tradition's understanding of following Jesus. At the Mennonite Church of Normal, this setting of Jesus' teaching was used for a summer series of worship services, each service taking up a different beatitude. One verse was added each week as the sermons and meditations guided the congregation through this biblical study. A similar approach could be adopted for teaching the beatitudes to children during bible school or to adults and teens at a weekend retreat. The song should be accompanied on piano and/or guitar. Soloists or a children's choir could emphasize a particular verse on a given week. "Blessed" could also be alternated with "Blest are they" by David Haas.

Breath in the wind

After a week spent working together on several musical collaborations, we stood in the Clemens's living room considering one last piece we might write. Jim began playing one of his Native American flutes. Dave stood looking at Coopers Mountain, visible from the window. The various images of God and God's work in the world—in both Creation and in human community—arrived easily and fit fluidly with the tune Jim composed. While God is not named directly in the piece, echoes from various scripture passages (such as the "still small voice" Elijah hears in 1 Kings 19: 11-12) anchor this hymn of praise within the Christian conviction that nature itself serves as a powerful revelation of God's presence and grace. Consider introducing the melody on an alto recorder or Native American flute. The hymn could also be meaningful as an opening for a service in an outdoor or camp setting. A choral arrangement for treble voices is available from Treble Clef Press (www.trebleclefpress.com/).

By the river, by the stream

Psalm 137 laments the separation of God's people from their homeland as they struggle to raise a familiar song in a time of grief and terror. Call and response in structure, the text uses rhetorical questions to demonstrate the difficulty of living through such times of corporate and individual exile. However, the tune always returns to the unison chorus, to the community supporting one another in song. The text also alludes to Psalm 1, where the psalmist asserts we are sustained like trees planted by the living water of God's love. We dedicate this hymn to Ken Nafziger, Marlene Kropf, and Marilyn Houser-Hamm who have inspired and cared for us (and countless other worshipers) during their many years of directing the annual Worship and Music Leaders weekend at Laurelville Mennonite Church Center in Pennsylvania.

Christ be with me

These familiar words, attributed to Saint Patrick, make an excellent benediction or a blessing for those leaving a congregation for temporary or long-term reasons. The meter, while a bit unconventional, follows the rhythm of the words. Sung lightly, not too fast, the hymn flows like a gentle dance.

Come make a noise

Few psalms have been set to music more often than Psalm 100. Like other settings, this one seeks to celebrate God not only with noise, but with purposeful sound—with song. The two parts, while not an actual canon, are similar and should be taught with some care. A leader could teach the congregation the upper line and a children's ensemble or small choir the second part. Transposing one or both lines for trumpet or horn can also support the singers. This setting represents one of our few collaborations for which the tune appeared before the adapted text.

Come to the table

Unlike "Jesus, offered up as bread" or "Pass this bread to your brother," which focus on the communion meal itself, "Come to the table" focuses on Christ's open invitation to come to his table as we are—loving, needy, and searching for truth. The melody emphasizes the open invitation, offering a tune easily grasped after a time or two through the hymn. Additional, suggested verses can be added as time allows and to highlight thematic concerns from the rest of the service. Finally, save the sending verse as a blessing for those leaving the communion table or for the service benediction.

Come! Walk in the light

This was originally composed as a song of response for Advent. The song also fits well as a response to other scripture readings or to prayer requests. The four-part a cappella response could be introduced by a choir and then sung by the congregation.

Come, brother, sit with me

In writing this hymn, we were affected by Michelle Hershberger's eloquent and challenging overview of the biblical practices and warrants for hospitality. In an issue of *Mennonite Life*, Hershberger points out that a basic feature of biblical hospitality is "the fluidity of the guest/host role. In the hospitality encounter, both host and guest are blessed, and both act as givers as well as receivers. This fluidity is supported in the ancient tongues. The word for host in Arabic (dayf), Greek (xenos), and Latin (hospes), also means guest." So this song exchanges gifts and roles as both parts sing an intertwining melody and countermelody. Hershberger's article can be read online (www.bethelks.edu/mennonitelife/2003Mar/hershberger.php). This hymn appeared in an issue of *Christian Reflections*, published by the Center for Christian Ethics at Baylor University (www.baylor.edu/christianethics/).

Gloria in excelsis deo

"Glory to God in the highest" sing the angels celebrating Christ's birth (Luke 2:8-14). As part of the Mass, the "Gloria" has been sung to a great variety of melodies. This shortened portion of the traditional text can be sung at Advent but also throughout the church year (excluding Lent for those congregations that abstain from singing "alleluia" until Easter).

Go, my friends, in grace

This functions as a sending song or benediction and can be sung by the congregation or offered as a blessing by a small choir or ensemble. The tune might also be exchanged between such groups (or between parts of the congregation) as a means of blessing one another. Notice that the final verse serves as an invitation to return to worship. A choral arrangement of this song is available from World Library Publications (www.wlpmusic.com).

God hears our cries *and* God who has saved

Though they can be used on their own, these two hymns were written to be sung after "While I keep silence," finishing an extended encounter with Psalm 32. Between hymns, it is appropriate to have portions of Psalm 32 read aloud, either responsively or by a liturgist. Leaving space for silence between songs also invites us to confess, to reflect on God's grace, and to prepare for the celebration of God's forgiveness and salvation. "God hears our cries" should be sung freely, following the shape of the musical and textual phrases. "God who has saved" works well as a round, literally demonstrating God's surrounding us with song.

Here in this body

This tune treats the eight-verse text as four double-length verses, creating an expansive, sweeping space to include all of us in the body of Christ. Because the text moves through the progression of age groups, distributing all or part of a verse to the appropriate group would be effective. Because this accompanied hymn will challenge many singers, it could be taught by a choir. (A healing service would be an ideal situation, with the choir singing the first three verses and the congregation joining on the final verse.)

Jesus, offered up as bread

The first hymn on which we collaborated, this communion song was initially conceived as a round and was sung in several congregational and seminary settings. Eastern Mennonite University choir director Ken Nafziger asked for a four-part arrangement to sing at a campus ceremony. When it came time to publish the hymn, we felt required to include both versions. For the round, it is often effective to sing the first verse in unison and begin the round on the second verse. A choir could sing the four-part version during communion. A string quartet can double the vocal lines to add a rich sonority. This hymn was originally published in *Sing the Journey: Hymnal: A Worship Book, Supplement I*. Scottdale, PA: Faith & Life, 2005.

Jesus calls us

"Jesus calls us" allows us to consider several direct invitations from Jesus. A rhythmic accompaniment on djembe adds to the movement of the vocal parts. Besides the several verses included, worship leaders might consider other phrases from Jesus' teachings that fit the rhythmic pattern and reinforce a particular worship or teaching focus (for instance, "Love your neighbor" or "Let the children").

Kyrie eleison

Sing this a cappella setting of the "Kyrie" as a response to congregational prayer requests, as a preparation for silent meditation, or as words of assurance after a period of confession. The first verse could be sung several times during a reading or prayer.

O God, be gracious

The first three verses of Psalm 67, arranged as a canon, serve as an invocation, as a call to prayer, or even as a benediction. When it comes time to end the round, singers should stop at the nearest fermata.

Oh, Abram, look up to the sky

To narrate the calling of Abram and Sarai from Genesis 12, we created a call and response that rehearses God's promises. A song leader/soloist can follow the written part closely or improvise a bit before inviting the congregation to sing the response. Rhythmic foot stomping can keep the piece moving. A worship leader can name the progression as Abram becomes Abraham and Sarai becomes Sarah, a progression that reinforces the biblical narrative. A children's choir or Sunday school/bible school class might also use this song in relation to lessons on God's promises.

Oh, sister, I beg you to listen to me

The tradition of Christian hymnody has always involved the setting of new lyrics to established tunes (and vice versa), giving familiar resonance to new lyrics and fresh energy to a known melody. This version of the tune EXPRESSION was transcribed at a *Sacred Harp* sing by George Pullen Jackson (*Another Sheaf of White Spirituals*, 1952). The Scotch snaps and raised sixths differ from the notated version in the *Original Sacred Harp*. These lyrics draw from the parable of the prodigal son and present a call to repentance. They also remind us of the Savior's intimate knowledge and love of each individual, even when we feel far from home. A choral arrangement of this tune was composed for a festival at Hesston College and is available from Table Round Press.

Open my ears, open my eyes

This is another hymn that invites God to inhabit and redeem our bodies. The volume and intensity of the singing should follow the lyrics as they build, gradually, to a full offering of our selves to God. The accompaniment leaves room for a skilled pianist to improvise and embellish the congregation's voices. The Eastern Mennonite University Chamber Singers included "Open my ears, open my eyes" as part of their 2005 repertoire.

Restore us, O God

Another song of response, this fits well in a service of confession or healing, and can be sung between individual scriptures or prayer requests. Having two or three different singers as leaders demonstrates the universal need of all believers to seek God's restoration.

Seek the peace of the city

In Jeremiah 29, the prophet speaks to the Israelites exiled in Babylon, instructing them to "Build houses and settle down; plant gardens and eat what they produce. Marry and have sons and daughters; find wives for your sons and give your daughters in marriage, so that they too may have sons and daughters. Increase in number there; do not decrease" (vv. 5-6). To a people in captivity, longing for their homeland, these commands must have surprised them. This hymn explores the contours of the prophet's words, reminding us that God's people are called to redeem the places we find ourselves, not to wait for some perfect day to be engaged with those around us. A song of peace, social justice, evangelism, and encouragement, the hymn reminds us that we are called not only to "seek the peace of the city" but also the welfare of the exile and the stranger.

Set your troubled hearts at rest

In John 14:1-7, Jesus comforts his disciples with the promise of both rest and a future home. Using these words as a template, this hymn also refers to other gospel passages, including Jesus' calming of the storm, his reminder that his yoke and burden are light, and his interaction with the doubting disciple Thomas. Effective when sung a cappella, the song can also be accompanied by various instruments. Exchanging the melody between parts or between ensemble and congregation can also allow time for listening and reflection, especially when this music is used for a healing service or as words of assurance after a time of confession. World Library Publications (www.wlpmusic.com) has published a choral arrangement of this song, including a part for C-instrument. This hymn arrangement is published with their permission.

Sing to the Lord of the harvest

Lombard Mennonite Church commissioned this piece for their 50th anniversary celebration in 2004, providing us with the phrase that became the hymn's title. Because this church (where we first worshiped and worked together) is an urban/suburban congregation, it seemed appropriate to be less literal with the bible's many agrarian images of God's provision, instead representing worship itself as a figurative "harvest of song." The music is in keeping with the expansive feel of the text. We are grateful to Camp Friendenswald's Summer Music Camp where we completed this hymn and first heard it sung by the camp's spirited young singers.

The smallest things

Adapting Matthew 6:28-30 for an accompanied gospel tune grew from inspiration provided by Alex Clemens. Alex came in from playing one day with some grasses he'd picked from the meadow near their home, and asked, "Dad, can you and Dave write a song about this?" A digital photo of Alex holding the grasses was sent, lyrics were returned via email, and a tune was born. Pianists should feel free to improvise in a gospel style. A choral arrangement was initially sung by the choir at Eastern Mennonite High School and is published by Choristers Guild (www.choristersguild.org). This version is presented with their permission.

Turn to me and answer

A straightforward prayer of the heart, the melody of this hymn can first be sung in unison and then sung multiple times as a canon. Like "Restore us, O God," or "O God, be gracious," the song can fit many places in a given service.

Wake us, Lord!

Written as an energetic table grace for music campers at Camp Friedenswald, "Wake us, Lord!" invites us to give our hands, our work, and our words over to God's purposes each day. At the start of Sunday school, bible school, or retreat/conference sessions, the piece might help to rouse singers in a fun, yet prayerful manner, getting them ready to participate more fully in worship and study. The rhythmic figures we suggest can be clapped, played on various drums or rhythm instruments, or tapped on tabletops with hands, spoons, or cups.

While I keep silence

An adaptation of Psalm 32, "While I keep silence" begins a pattern of confession, repentance, assurance, and celebration that continues with "God hears our cries" and concludes with "God who has saved." A brief service including this sequence appears in this volume. Sing the melody fairly slowly and plaintively to emphasize the rests after "silence" and the descending slurs at the end of the verse, which use word painting to underscore the psalmist's grief over sin. The song should be sung a cappella, though it can be played on a solo instrument (viola or cello might work well) as music for meditation earlier in the service or following a reading of Psalm 32.

A Brief Service of Praise*

Inviting God

Wake us, Lord!
As we rise, O God, to meet you
Open my ears, open my eyes
Come! Walk in the light

Praising God

Come make a noise
Sing to the Lord of the harvest
Gloria in excelsis deo!

Thanking God

God who has saved
The smallest things
Come, brother, sit with me

Celebrating God's Presence

Breath in the wind
Here in this body

Walking with God

Go, my friends, in grace
Restore us, O God

* We offer these brief outlines to spur the creativity of congregations and worship leaders. The order and number of hymns suggested for these services should be adjusted and supplemented to meet the season, spiritual needs, time constraints, and musical abilities of any given congregation. Scripture passages, prayers, and brief rituals should also be inserted where appropriate.

A Brief Service of Jesus' Teachings and Presence*

Jesus' Teaching

Jesus calls us
Blessed
The smallest things

Jesus' Invitation and Sacrifice

Oh, sister, I beg you to listen to me
Come to the table
Jesus, offered up as bread
Pass this bread to your brother

Jesus' Promises and Comfort

Set your troubled hearts at rest

Jesus' Presence and Blessing

Christ be with me

* The notes and the scriptural index provide biblical references to read between hymns. Brief gospel passages could also be printed in a bulletin for meditation. If communion is celebrated, consider having an ensemble sing "Jesus, offered up as bread" or "Pass this bread to your brother" while the meal is served. The Lord's Prayer can also be recited between sections two and three or sections three and four.

A Brief Service of Healing*

Invocation

As we rise, O God, to meet you (vv. 1-4)
Open my ears, open my eyes
Oh, sister, I beg you to listen to me

Lamentation/Confession

By the river, by the stream
Here in this body
While I keep silence
Turn to me and answer
Kyrie eleison

Forgiveness/Assurance

God hears our cries
God who has saved
O God, be gracious
Restore us, O God
Set your troubled hearts at rest

Sending/Blessing

As we rise, O God, to meet you (v. 5)
Go, my friends, in grace
Christ be with me
Come! Walk in the light

* Songs can be included or omitted from each section depending on other aspects of this service. For instance, if a call to worship is used, the invocation might be left out. If anointing or prayer is offered to individuals, either the lamentation or forgiveness sections could include several hymns.

A Brief Service of Psalms*

Praise (Orientation)

Come make a noise (Psalm 100)
O God, be gracious (Psalm 67)
Come! Walk in the light (Psalm 89:15)

Follow the singing here with an antiphonal or dramatic reading of a psalm of praise, such as Psalms 8, 98, 103, or 113.

Lament and Confession (Disorientation)

By the river, by the stream (Psalm 137)
Turn to me and answer (Psalm 54)
While I keep silence (Psalm 32)

Begin or end this section by reading a psalm of either community or individual lament, crying out to God. Corporate laments might include Psalms 12, 44, 60, 74, 79, 80, 83, 85, 90, 94, 123, 126, 129. Individual laments could include Psalms 3, 4, 5, 7, 9-10, 13, 14, 17, 22, 25, 26, 27, 28, 31, 39, 40:12-17, 41, 42-43, 53, 54-56, 57, 59, 61, 64, 69, 70, 71, 77, 86, 89, 120, 139, 141, 142. For individual confession, consider Psalms 6, 32, 38, 51, 102, 130, 143.

Salvation and Celebration (Reorientation)

God hears our cries (Psalm 32)
God who has saved (Psalm 32)
O God, be gracious (Psalm 67)
Restore us, O God (Psalm 80)
Come make a noise (Psalm 100)

Consider using the words from one of the above songs as either a sung or spoken benediction for this service, emphasizing the redemptive and celebratory acts of God.

* The order of this service borrows from scholar Walter Brueggemann's *Spirituality of the Psalms* (Minneapolis: Augsburg/Fortress, 2001) and his earlier *The Message of the Psalms* (Minneapolis: Augsburg, 1984). Brueggemann describes three categories for understanding the Hebrew psalter as it shows the range of human encounters with God. We begin with psalms of orientation, those moments when we feel confidence and assurance in God's presence, when we find ourselves celebrating and relying on God's goodness. Then there are psalms of disorientation, when we must be honest about our anger, confusion, brokenness, sin, and loss, both corporately and individually. Finally, we find psalms that restore and reorient us, that, in Breuggemann's words, "speak boldly about a new gift from God, a fresh intrusion that makes all things new" (*Message 19*). We are indebted to John Bell for alerting us to Breuggemann's work and for challenging us to especially consider writing songs of lament.

Musical Voicings

UNISON, a cappella

Breath in the wind
God hears our cries
Oh, Abram, look up to the sky
While I keep silence

UNISON, accompanied

Blessed
Come to the table
Come! Walk in the light
Jesus, offered up as bread

TWO-PART, a cappella

Come, brother, sit with me
Come make a noise

TWO-PART, accompanied

As we rise, O God, to meet you

FOUR-PART, a cappella

Christ be with me
Come! Walk in the light
Go, my friends, in grace
Jesus, offered up as bread
Kyrie eleison
Oh, sister, I beg you to listen to me
Pass this bread to your brother
Seek the peace of the city
Set your troubled hearts at rest
Sing to the Lord of the harvest

FOUR-PART, accompanied

Here in this body
Open my ears, open my eyes
The smallest things

CANON

Breath in the wind
Come! Walk in the light
God who has saved
Jesus, offered up as bread
O God, be gracious
Turn to me and answer
Wake us, Lord!

CALL & RESPONSE

By the river, by the stream
Gloria in excelsis deo
God hears our cries
Jesus calls us
Oh, Abram, look up to the sky
Restore us, O God

Themes and Uses in Worship

Benediction/Blessing

As we rise, O God, to meet you (v. 5)
Christ be with me
Come to the table (v. 4)
Come! Walk in the light
Go, my friends, in grace

Community/Hospitality

Come, brother, sit with me
Here in this body
Pass this bread to your brother

Communion

As we rise, O God, to meet you
Come, brother, sit with me
Come to the table
Jesus, offered up as bread
Pass this bread to your brother

Confession/Repentance

As we rise, O God, to meet you
Here in this body
Kyrie eleison
Oh, sister, I beg you to listen to me
Restore us, O God
Turn to me and answer
While I keep silence

Creation

As we rise, O God, to meet you
Breath in the wind
The smallest things

Forgiveness and Assurance

God hears our cries
God who has saved
O God, be gracious
Restore us, O God
Set your troubled hearts at rest

Gathering

As we rise, O God, to meet you
Come! Walk in the light
Open my ears, open my eyes
Wake us, Lord!

God's Promises

Oh, Abram, look up to the sky
Set your troubled hearts at rest

Justice/Peace

By the river, by the stream
Here in this body
Seek the peace of the city
Sing to the Lord of the harvest

Lament/Healing

By the river, by the stream
Christ be with me
Here in this body
Open my ears, open my eyes
Set your troubled hearts at rest
Turn to me and answer
While I keep silence

Praise

Breath in the wind
Come make a noise
God who has saved
Gloria in excelsis deo!
Sing to the Lord of the harvest
The smallest things

Thanksgiving

Breath in the wind
Come, brother, sit with me
Come make a noise
God who has saved
Sing to the Lord of the harvest
The smallest things

Scriptural References

Genesis 2:4-7
As we rise, O God, to meet you

Genesis 12:1-4
Oh, Abram, look up to the sky

Deuteronomy 10:19
Come, brother, sit with me
Seek the peace of the city

1 Kings 19:11-12
Breath in the wind

Isaiah 2:5
Come! Walk in the light

Isaiah 43:1
Oh, sister, I beg you to listen to me

Jeremiah 29:4-14
Seek the peace of the city

Psalm 32
While I keep silence
God hears our cries
God who has saved

Psalm 89:15
Come! Walk in the light

Psalm 100
Come make a noise

Psalm 137
By the river, by the stream

Matthew 5:3-12
Blessed

Matthew 6:28-30
The smallest things

Matthew 9:38
Sing to the Lord of the harvest

Matthew 26:20-29
As we rise, O God, to meet you
Jesus, offered up as bread
Pass this bread to your brother

Mark 4:35-41
Set your troubled hearts at rest

Mark 14:17-25
As we rise, O God, to meet you
Come to the table
Jesus, offered up as bread
Pass this bread to your brother

Luke 2: 8-9; 13-14
Gloria in excelsis deo!

Luke 6:20-26
Blessed

Luke 10:1-2
Sing to the Lord of the harvest

Luke 10:38-42
Come, brother, sit with me

Luke 22:14-38
As we rise, O God, to meet you
Come to the table
Jesus, offered up as bread
Pass this bread to your brother

Luke 24:13-35
Seek the peace of the city

John 6:48-58
As we rise, O God, to meet you
Come to the table
Jesus, offered up as bread
Pass this bread to your brother

John 14:1-2
Set your troubled hearts at rest

John 20:24-29
Set your troubled heart at rest

Romans 12:4-5
Here in this body

1 Corinthians 11:24-25
As we rise, O God, to meet you
Come to the table
Jesus, offered up as bread
Pass this bread to your brother

1 Corinthians 12:12-26
Here in this body

Hebrews 13:2
Come, brother, sit with me

1 John 1:7
Come! Walk in the light

Revelation 21:1-5
Here in this body

Acknowledgments

For permission to include the following hymns, we are grateful to:

World Library Publications (www.wlpmusic.com): "Set your troubled hearts at rest."
Catalog Number: 008819

Choristers Guild (www.choristersguild.org): "The smallest things."
Catalog Number: CGA1106.

A portion of the introduction initially appeared as "Sharing in the Muse: Friendship, Artistic Creation, and the Church." *Leader* 2.4 (2005): 5-6.

We thank Mennonite congregations in Lombard, IL, Normal, IL, Urbana, IL, and Harrisonburg, VA for nurturing our collaborative work and for trying out many of these hymns when they were first written. We're thankful as well to Hal Hess and the staff and singers at Camp Friedenswald's Summer Music Camp for inviting us to be artists in residence. Goshen College, Hesston College, Associated Mennonite Biblical Seminary, Wheaton College, Eastern Mennonite High School, and, especially, Eastern Mennonite University and their Chamber Singers have all been supportive in various ways, as have the staff and attendees at the Laurelville Music and Worship Leaders weekends.

Many other individuals (too many to mention) have supported our work and made specific suggestions about particular hymns. Alice Parker and Mary Oyer responded to this collection generously, as did Ken Medema. We owe a special thanks to Ken Nafziger, whose challenging and practical advice has improved many of these pieces.

Our greatest gratitude goes to our families, who have been supportive in tangible and intangible ways. Angie Clemens was the first to hear and lead many of these songs, offering not only her enthusiasm but also a gentle, critical ear. And, of course, thanks to Alex and Lena Clemens, and Hannah and Ethan Wright, for singing.